KEEP IT SIMPLE, *Y'all*

KEEP IT SIMPLE, Y'all

Easy Dinners from Your Barefoot Neighbor

MATTHEW BOUNDS

Clarkson Potter / Publishers

New York

Copyright © 2024 by Matthew Bounds

Published in the United States by Clarkson Potter/Publishers, an imprint of the Crown Publishing Group, a division of Penguin Random House LLC, New York.
clarksonpotter.com

Penguin Random House values and supports copyright. Copyright fuels creativity, encourages diverse voices, promotes free speech, and creates a vibrant culture. Thank you for buying an authorized edition of this book and for complying with copyright laws by not reproducing, scanning, or distributing any part of it in any form without permission. You are supporting writers and allowing Penguin Random House to continue to publish books for every reader. Please note that no part of this book may be used or reproduced in any manner for the purpose of training artificial intelligence technologies or systems.

CLARKSON POTTER is a trademark and POTTER with colophon is a registered trademark of Penguin Random House LLC.

Library of Congress Control Number: 2024944986

FRONTIS: Chicken Cobbler, recipe page 131

ISBN: 979-8-217-03415-4

Ebook ISBN: 979-8-217-03416-1

Printed in Canada

10 9 8 7 6 5 4 3 2 1

First Edition

Contents

Introduction 7

Low 'n Slow 8
Chicken and Wild Rice 11
Creamy Mushroom Chicken 13
Honey Garlic Chicken 15
Beef Stew 17
Beef and Mushroom Stroganoff 19
Hawaiian Pork 21
Pork and Mushroom Marsala 23
Coconut Curry Chicken 25
Beef and Mushroom Risotto 27
Chicken Stew 29
Lemon Sun-Dried Tomato Chicken 31
Chicken Pita Wraps 33
Smothered Cube Steak and Onions 35
Chicken Tinga Tacos 37
Chicken Tortilla Soup 39
Carnitas 41
Chicken Cacciatore 43
Beef and Broccoli 45
Pork and Cauliflower Curry 47
Beef Chili 49

Sheet Pan Dinners 50
Shrimp and Veggie Stir-Fry 53
BBQ Chicken with Corn on the Cob 55
Lemon Dijon Salmon and Veggies 57
Italian Chicken with Zesty Veggies 59
Chicken Veggie Bake 61
Pork and Pineapple Skewers 63
Shrimp Boil 65
Beef Fajitas 67
Parmesan Ranch Pork Chops 69
Coconut Lime Shrimp and Quinoa 71
Chipotle Lime Chicken Drumsticks 73
Maple Dijon Glazed Chicken 75
Sausage and Gnocchi 77
Spicy Peanut Chicken 79
Cajun Ranch Chicken Breasts 81
Honey Dijon Drumsticks 83

One-Pot Meals 84
Chorizo Chicken Skillet 87
Kinda Sorta Chicken Alfredo 89
Broccoli Cheese Orzo 91
Sun-Dried Tomato Chicken 93
Pork Rice 95
Breakfast Skillet 97
Beef and Rice 99
Onion Butter Steak and Potatoes 101
Goat Cheese Gnocchi and
Meatball Soup 103
Italian Sausage Rigatoni 105
Taco Taters 107
Creamy Lemon Shrimp Orzo 109
Cajun Ranch Chicken Sausage Pasta 111

Rotisserie Realness 112
Chicken and Stuffing 115
Cheat Chicken Chili 117
French Onion Chicken Casserole 119
Spinach Alfredo Lasagna Rolls 121
Chicken Parmesan Casserole 123
Goat Cheese Pesto Pasta 125
Chicken Pot Pie 127

Come Fix You a Plate 128
Chicken Cobbler 131
Chicken and Dumplin's 133
Cajun't Chicken Pasta 135
"Really Nice" Salisbury Steak 137
Myrtle's Pasta Bake 139
CJ's Pork Chops in Onion Gravy 141

Acknowledgments 142
Index 143

Introduction

Even the best home cooks fall into a rut sometimes and need a bit of inspiration for something new. I hope you find that here. Many of us are busy and don't have time to scroll endlessly online looking for dinner ideas. I aim to take some of the pressure off with the recipes in this book. Plenty of folks, like me, never learned to cook growing up, and we deserve a hot, delicious meal, too. For that reason, I tried my best to write out all the instructions in simple, easy-to-follow terms. And then, there are my friends who can cook dinner but don't enjoy it. That's okay, I gotcha covered. Throw it in the slow cooker and go on about your day. It'll be ready in 6 to 8 hours.

As you work your way through this book, you'll notice patterns emerge. You'll begin to pick up on the rhythm of one-pot meals, the basics of a slow cooker, and the fundamentals of a sheet pan dinner. Once you understand the principles, the ingredients don't matter so much, and you're free to go wild and experiment with flavors you enjoy. If you follow me on social media, then you know that I treat recipes as suggestions, and I want you to do the same with this book. Nothing makes me happier than when people show me a recipe of mine that they cooked with their own tweaks and modifications. Go ham, y'all!

My wish is that this book is a helpful tool, and that together we can make dinnertime just a little bit easier.

Low 'n Slow

This entire collection of recipes can be placed directly in the slow cooker, with no stovetop action required! If you have the time and choose to, you can certainly put a little sear on the meat beforehand, but it's not necessary.

Feel free to swap out the protein and vegetables in these dishes. My recipe calls for pork loin, but you've got a pack of chicken that needs to be used up? Change it out! Don't like carrots? Leave them out or use another vegetable instead. There are no rules here.

I tried to refrain from using as much cream cheese and cream of something soups that slow cooker recipes trend toward, but if you think one of these dishes could be improved by adding cream of chicken or a block of cheese, go for it!

Remember, this is your kitchen and your dinner. Cook food you enjoy.

Chicken and Wild Rice

This is the perfect recipe to curl up with on a cold, gloomy day.
It's rich, creamy, and oh so comforting!

 Prep Time: 15 mins
Cook Time: 3 to 4 hrs high
                6 to 8 hrs low

 6 to 8 Servings

- 2 to 3 boneless, skinless chicken breasts
- 1 cup wild rice
- 1 onion, diced
- 2 large carrots, peeled and diced (or 1 pound baby carrots)
- 2 celery ribs, sliced
- Minced garlic, to taste
- 4 cups chicken broth
- 1 teaspoon each, dried thyme and rosemary
- ½ teaspoon dried sage
- Salt and pepper, to taste
- 1 cup heavy cream

1 Place the chicken in the slow cooker, and add the rice, onion, carrots, celery, and garlic on top.

2 Pour over the broth and seasonings, and gently stir to combine.

3 Cover and cook on high for 3 to 4 hours, or on low for 6 to 8 hours.

4 Once cooked, shred the chicken (remove to do this if you prefer, and add back to the slow cooker).

5 Add the cream, and taste for seasoning. Cover and cook for another half hour on low.

Quick Tip: If you don't care for shredded chicken, or simply don't want to bother with doing it, cut the chicken up into bite-size pieces before cooking.

Creamy Mushroom Chicken

 Prep Time: 15 mins
Cook Time: 3 to 4 hrs high
            6 to 8 hrs low

 4 to 6 Servings

- 2 to 3 boneless chicken breasts, cut into bite-size pieces
- 8 ounces sliced mushrooms
- 1 diced onion
- Minced garlic, to taste
- Italian seasoning, to taste
- Salt and pepper, to taste
- 1 can (10.5 ounces) cream of mushroom soup
- 1 cup chicken stock
- 1 cup sour cream
- 1 pound cooked short pasta of your choice

1 Stir together the chicken, mushrooms, onions, and seasonings in the slow cooker.

2 In a separate bowl, mix together the soup and chicken stock. Pour this over everything in the slow cooker and stir to combine.

3 Cover and cook on high for 3 hours, or low for 6 to 8 hours.

4 During the last half hour of cooking, stir in the sour cream.

5 Serve over the pasta, or add the cooked pasta to the slow cooker and mix together before serving.

Honey Garlic Chicken

This chicken is sticky, tangy, and tender!

 Prep Time: 10 mins
Cook Time: 3 to 4 hrs high
6 to 8 hrs low

 4 to 6 Servings

- 2 to 3 boneless chicken breasts, cut into bite-size pieces
- ½ cup honey
- ¼ cup soy sauce
- Minced garlic, to taste
- 1 tablespoon rice vinegar
- 1 tablespoon sesame oil
- Cornstarch slurry (2 tablespoons of cornstarch with 2 tablespoons of water, mixed)
- Cooked rice
- Sesame seeds and sliced green onions, for garnish

1 Place the chicken breasts pieces in the slow cooker.

2 In a bowl, whisk together the honey, soy sauce, garlic, vinegar, and sesame oil.

3 Pour the mixture over the chicken and stir to combine.

4 Cover and cook on high for 3 to 4 hours, or low for 6 to 8 hours.

5 During the last half hour of cooking, stir in the cornstarch slurry to thicken the sauce (you'll need to cook this on high if you aren't already).

6 Serve over cooked rice (I like jasmine) and garnish with green onions and sesame seeds.

Quick Tip: Add broccoli florets, green beans, or vegetables of your choice.

15

Beef Stew

Hearty, savory, and sure to be enjoyed by everyone at dinner!

Prep Time: 20 mins
Cook Time: 4 to 6 hrs high
8 to 10 hrs low

6 to 8 Servings

- 2 pounds beef stew meat
- 1 onion, diced
- 4 carrots, peeled and sliced, or 1 pound of baby carrots
- 3 celery ribs, sliced
- 2 potatoes, peeled and diced, or 1 pound of baby potatoes, cut in halves
- 1 cup frozen peas
- 4 cups beef broth
- Minced garlic, to taste
- Salt and pepper, to taste
- 2 tablespoons tomato paste
- 2 tablespoons Worcestershire sauce
- 1 teaspoon each dried thyme and rosemary, or a packet of your favorite beef stew seasoning mix
- 1 large bay leaf, or 2 smaller ones
- Cornstarch slurry (2 tablespoons of cornstarch with 2 tablespoons of water, mixed)

1. Place the beef and all vegetables in the slow cooker. Salt and pepper everything and toss to coat.

2. In a separate bowl, whisk together the broth, tomato paste, Worcestershire, and seasonings. Pour this over everything in the slow cooker.

3. Add the bay leaf on top.

4. Cover and cook on high for 4 to 6 hours, or on low for 8 to 10 hours.

5. During the last half hour of cooking, stir in the cornstarch slurry to thicken (you'll need to cook this on high, if you aren't already).

6. Pull the bay leaf out and throw it away, and taste for seasoning.

7. Serve by itself, over rice, or with some thick-sliced crusty bread.

Beef and Mushroom Stroganoff

Comfort food at its finest!

 Prep Time: 15 mins
Cook Time: 3 to 4 hrs high
6 to 8 hrs low

 6 to 8 Servings

- 2 pounds beef stew meat
- 1 onion, diced
- 16 ounces mushrooms, sliced
- Minced garlic, to taste
- Salt and pepper, to taste
- 1 cup beef broth (or one 10.5-ounce can)
- 2 tablespoons Worcestershire
- 2 tablespoons Dijon mustard
- 1 teaspoon dried thyme (if you have it on hand)
- 1 cup sour cream
- Cooked egg noodles or mashed potatoes, whichever you prefer

1   Place the beef, onion, mushrooms, garlic, and salt and pepper in the slow cooker, stirring to combine.

2   In a separate bowl, whisk together the broth, Worcestershire, mustard, and thyme.

3   Pour the mixture over everything in the slow cooker and stir together.

4   Cover and cook on high for 3 to 4 hours, or on low for 6 to 8 hours. During the last half hour of cooking, stir in the sour cream.

5   Serve over the egg noodles or mashed potatoes.

Quick Tip: If you'd like your sauce a bit thicker, add a cornstarch slurry with the sour cream. I'd start with 1 tablespoon of cornstarch and 1 tablespoon of water and see how you like it. If you do this, you'll need to cook it on high to properly thicken. You can replace the broth, mustard, and thyme with a can of condensed cream of golden mushroom soup if you'd like.

Hawaiian Pork

Sweet and salty, this dish is great for a summer evening!

 Prep Time: 15 mins
Cook Time: 3 to 4 hrs high
6 to 8 hrs low

 6 to 8 Servings

- 1 can (20 ounces) pineapple chunks, with the juice
- 1 red bell pepper, diced
- 1 onion, diced
- Minced garlic, to taste
- ½ cup soy sauce
- ¼ cup ketchup
- ¼ cup brown sugar
- 2 tablespoons rice vinegar
- 1 tablespoon sesame oil
- 1 tablespoon dried ground ginger
- 1 teaspoon onion powder
- 1 teaspoon garlic powder
- 1 teaspoon black pepper
- 2 pounds pork loin, trimmed and cut into bite-size pieces
- Cornstarch slurry (2 tablespoons of cornstarch with 2 tablespoons of water, mixed)
- Sesame seeds and sliced green onions, for garnish
- Cooked rice

1 In the slow cooker, mix together the pineapple, bell pepper, onion, garlic, soy sauce, ketchup, brown sugar, vinegar, sesame oil, ginger, onion and garlic powder, and pepper until well combined.

2 Add the pork loin pieces and stir to coat with the sauce.

3 Cover and cook on high for 3 to 4 hours, or on low for 6 to 8 hours.

4 During the last half hour, stir in the cornstarch slurry (you'll need to cook this on high, if you aren't already). If you prefer a thicker sauce, double the slurry.

5 Serve over rice (I like jasmine) and garnish with the green onions and sesame seeds.

Pork and Mushroom Marsala

 Prep Time: 15 mins
Cook Time: 3 to 4 hrs high
6 to 8 hrs low

 4 to 6 Servings

- 2 pounds pork loin, cut into thick slices
- 8 ounces mushrooms, sliced
- 1 onion, sliced
- Minced garlic, to taste
- 1 teaspoon dried thyme
- Salt and pepper, to taste
- 1 cup Marsala cooking wine
- 2 tablespoons butter
- Cornstarch slurry (2 tablespoons of cornstarch with 2 tablespoons of water, mixed)
- Mashed potatoes

1. Place the pork, mushrooms, onion, garlic, and seasonings in the slow cooker and stir to combine.

2. Pour the wine over everything.

3. Cook on high for 3 to 4 hours, or low for 6 to 8 hours.

4. Remove the pork loin and set aside. Add 2 tablespoons of butter to the slow cooker and stir together until smooth, then add a cornstarch slurry and cook on high for another half hour (you can add the pork loin back in after you add the butter and cornstarch slurry).

5. Serve with mashed potatoes.

Quick Tip: For my friends in recovery, use chicken stock in place of the wine. It'll be just as tasty. I'm really proud of you. Keep it up!

23

Coconut Curry Chicken

Warm, savory curry combined with creamy coconut milk makes this dish a star!

 Prep Time: 20 mins
Cook Time: 3 to 4 hrs high
6 to 8 hrs low

 4 to 6 Servings

- 1.5 pounds boneless, skinless chicken thighs, cut into bite-size pieces
- 1 onion, diced
- Minced garlic, to taste
- 1 red bell pepper, sliced
- 2 carrots, peeled and sliced
- 1 pound baby potatoes, cut into halves
- 1 can (13.5 ounces) coconut milk
- 3 tablespoons red curry paste
- 2 tablespoons soy sauce
- 1 tablespoon brown sugar
- 1 tablespoon curry powder
- 1 teaspoon ground ginger
- ½ teaspoon turmeric powder
- Salt and pepper, to taste
- Cooked rice and/or naan

1 Place the chicken, onion, garlic, bell pepper, carrots, and potatoes in the slow cooker.

2 In a separate bowl, whisk together the coconut milk, curry paste, soy sauce, brown sugar, curry powder, ginger, turmeric, and salt and pepper.

3 Pour the mixture over everything in the slow cooker and stir together.

4 Cover and cook on high for 3 to 4 hours, or on low for 6 to 8 hours.

5 Serve over rice or with naan, or both.

Quick Tip: If you want a spicier curry, consider adding chili powder, cayenne, or crushed red pepper to this dish.

Beef and Mushroom Risotto

Prep Time: 10 mins
Cook Time: 3 to 4 hrs high
6 to 8 hrs low

4 to 6 Servings

- 1 to 2 pounds beef stew meat
- 1 onion, diced
- Minced garlic, to taste
- 8 ounces mushrooms, sliced
- 5 cups beef broth
- 1 teaspoon dried thyme
- Salt and pepper, to taste
- 2 cups arborio rice
- ½ cup grated Parmesan cheese
- 2 tablespoons butter

1 Place the beef, onion, garlic, mushrooms, broth, and seasonings in the slow cooker and stir to combine.

2 Cover and cook on high for 3 to 4 hours, or low for 6 to 8 hours.

3 Add the rice and stir together. Cover and cook for another 45 minutes to 1 hour on high.

4 Add the butter and Parmesan cheese and mix until smooth and melted. The risotto should have a creamy consistency. If it's too thick, stir in some additional broth or cream to loosen it.

Chicken Stew

Prep Time: 20 mins
Cook Time: 3 to 4 hrs high
6 to 8 hrs low

4 to 6 Servings

- 1.5 pounds boneless, skinless chicken thighs, cut into bite-size pieces
- 4 carrots, peeled and sliced (or 1 pound baby carrots)
- 3 celery ribs, sliced
- 1 onion, diced
- 2 potatoes, peeled and diced (or 1 pound baby potatoes, cut into halves)
- 1 cup frozen peas
- Minced garlic, to taste
- 4 cups chicken broth
- 2 teaspoons dried thyme
- Salt and pepper, to taste
- 2 bay leaves
- Cornstarch slurry (2 tablespoons of cornstarch with 2 tablespoons of water, mixed)

1 Add all ingredients, except the cornstarch slurry, to the slow cooker and stir to combine.

2 Cover and cook on high for 3 to 4 hours, or low for 6 to 8 hours.

3 If you prefer a thicker stew, add the cornstarch slurry during the last half hour, or stir in one 10.5-ounce can of cream of chicken or cream of mushroom soup. If you add the slurry, you'll need to turn the slow cooker to high if you haven't already.

4 Serve over cooked rice if you prefer.

Lemon Sun-Dried Tomato Chicken

Tangy citrus and sweet sun-dried tomatoes over angel hair pasta makes this dish bright and sunny!

 Prep Time: 10 mins
Cook Time: 3 to 4 hrs high
6 to 8 hrs low

 4 to 6 Servings

- 2 to 3 boneless, skinless chicken breasts
- 4 to 5 ounces sun-dried tomatoes, chopped
- Minced garlic, to taste
- Juice of 2 lemons
- 2 tablespoons olive oil
- 2 teaspoons Italian seasoning
- ½ teaspoon paprika
- Salt and pepper, to taste
- ½ cup chicken broth
- 1 lemon, cut into round slices
- 1 cup chicken broth
- 1 cup heavy cream
- 12 ounces angel hair pasta, uncooked
- Grated Parmesan cheese, for serving (optional)

1 Place the chicken and tomatoes in the slow cooker.

2 Mix together the garlic, lemon juice, olive oil, seasoning, and broth together. Pour over the chicken.

3 Lay 1 lemon slice on top of each chicken breast.

4 Cover and cook on high for 3 to 4 hours, or on low for 6 to 8 hours.

5 Remove the chicken breasts and shred. Discard the lemon slices.

6 Pour the additional cup of chicken broth and cream in the slow cooker, stirring to combine with the liquid already there.

7 Put the angel hair into the bottom of the slow cooker and return the chicken, laying it on top of the pasta.

8 Cook on high for half an hour, stirring halfway through, so that the pasta doesn't stick.

9 Toss everything together and serve. If the pasta is too dry, add a bit of water to thin it out. Top with grated Parmesan cheese if you like.

Chicken Pita Wraps

Prep Time: 15 mins
Cook Time: 3 to 4 hrs high
6 to 8 hrs low

4 to 6 Servings

- 1.5 pounds boneless, skinless chicken thighs
- Salt and pepper, to taste
- 1 onion, thinly sliced
- 1 red bell pepper, thinly sliced
- 1 yellow bell pepper, thinly sliced
- ½ cup pitted Kalamata olives, chopped
- 4 to 5 ounces sun-dried tomatoes, chopped
- Minced garlic, to taste
- 1 tablespoon Italian seasoning
- Juice of 2 lemons
- Tzatziki sauce
- Feta cheese crumbles
- Pita bread

1   Season the chicken thighs with salt and pepper and place them in the slow cooker in a single layer.

2   Add the Italian seasoning, additional salt and pepper, and vegetables over the chicken.

3   Sprinkle the lemon juice over everything.

4   Cover and cook on high for 3 to 4 hours or low for 6 to 8 hours.

5   Shred the chicken, and mix it with the vegetables.

6   Warm the pita bread and spread a layer of Tzatziki sauce over it, then spoon over the chicken and vegetable mixture. Top with feta crumbles and serve.

Smothered Cube Steak and Onions

Soft onions, fork-tender steak, and a delicious gravy. What's not to love?

 Prep Time: 15 mins
Cook Time: 3 to 4 hrs high
6 to 8 hrs low

 4 Servings

- 2 pounds cube steak
- Dijon mustard
- Salt and pepper, to taste
- 2 onions, thinly sliced
- ¼ cup Worcestershire sauce
- 1 packet onion soup mix

1 Salt and pepper the meat, then spread a layer of mustard over one side. Place it in the slow cooker, mustard side down (it will probably overlap a bit, and that's okay).

2 Spread the onions over the cube steak in an even layer.

3 Sprinkle the onion soup mix over the onions, then drizzle the Worcestershire sauce over everything.

4 Cover and cook on high for 3 to 4 hours, or low for 6 to 8 hours, stirring the onions about halfway through.

5 Serve with mashed potatoes.

Quick Tip: For a thicker, creamier gravy, add a can of cream of mushroom soup over the top when you begin cooking. Or, for a thicker sauce, add a cornstarch slurry to the onions and cook on high for an additional 30 minutes (remove the steak, stir the slurry into the sauce until fully incorporated, then add the steak back to the slow cooker).

Chicken Tinga Tacos

Prep Time: 15 mins
Cook Time: 3 to 4 hrs high
6 to 8 hrs low

4 to 6 Servings

- 2 pounds boneless, skinless chicken breasts
- 1 onion, thinly sliced
- Salt and pepper, to taste
- Minced garlic, to taste
- 1 can (14 ounces) diced tomatoes
- 3 chipotle peppers in adobo sauce, chopped
- 1 tablespoon adobo sauce, from the chipotle peppers can
- 1 teaspoon cumin
- 1 teaspoon dried oregano
- 1 teaspoon smoked paprika
- ½ teaspoon chili powder
- Corn or flour tortillas

1 Salt and pepper the chicken and place in the slow cooker with the onion slices on top.

2 In a separate bowl, mix together the garlic, tomatoes, peppers, adobo sauce, cumin, oregano, paprika, and chili powder.

3 Pour the mixture over the chicken and onions.

4 Cover and cook on high for 3 to 4 hours, or low for 6 to 8 hours.

5 Shred the chicken and mix it with the sauce.

6 Serve in warm tortillas with your favorite toppings!

Quick Tip: Use a packet of taco seasoning mix in place of the cumin, oregano, paprika, and chili powder.

Chicken Tortilla Soup

 Prep Time: 15 mins
Cook Time: 3 to 4 hrs high
6 to 8 hrs low

 4 to 6 Servings

- 1 pound boneless, skinless chicken breasts
- Salt and pepper, to taste
- 1 can (15 ounces) black beans, drained and rinsed
- 1 can (15 ounces) diced tomatoes, with the juice
- 1 can (4 ounces) diced green chilies
- 1 onion, diced
- 1 bell pepper (any color), diced
- 1 cup frozen corn kernels
- 3 cups chicken broth
- Juice of 1 lime
- 1 teaspoon chili powder
- 1 teaspoon cumin
- 1 teaspoon garlic powder
- ½ teaspoon smoked paprika
- ½ teaspoon oregano
- 8 ounces cream cheese, softened
- Tortilla chips or strips

1 Place the chicken, salt and pepper, black beans, tomatoes, green chilies, onion, bell pepper, and corn in the slow cooker.

2 Pour in the chicken broth and lime juice.

3 Add the dry seasonings and stir to combine.

4 Cook on high for 3 to 4 hours, or on low for 6 to 8 hours.

5 Shred the chicken, then add the cream cheese and allow it to cook until melted. Mix to fully incorporate with the soup.

6 Serve with your favorite toppings and enjoy!

Quick Tip: In place of the chili powder, cumin, garlic powder, paprika, and oregano, use a packet of taco seasoning mix.

Carnitas

 Prep Time: 15 mins
Cook Time: 4 to 6 hrs high
8 to 10 hrs low

 4 to 6 Servings

- 3 to 4 pounds pork shoulder or butt
- 1 tablespoon chili powder
- 1 teaspoon ground cumin
- 1 teaspoon dried oregano
- 1 teaspoon smoked paprika
- ½ teaspoon ground coriander
- ½ teaspoon each of salt and pepper, or to taste
- 1 onion, diced
- Minced garlic, to taste
- Juice of 2 oranges
- Juice of 1 lime
- 2 bay leaves (3 if they're smaller)
- Corn or flour tortillas

1 Cut the pork into large chunks and trim off the excess fat. Place it into a bowl and add the chili powder, cumin, oregano, paprika, coriander, and salt and pepper and mix it really well. You want to get the pork fully coated in the seasoning.

2 Place the onion and garlic in the slow cooker, then add the pork on top.

3 Pour over the orange and lime juice, and then add the bay leaves on top.

4 Cover and cook on high for 4 to 6 hours, or on low for 8 to 10 hours.

5 Remove the bay leaves and shred the pork, then mix with the juices.

6 Serve on warm tortillas with your favorite toppings!

Chicken Cacciatore

Rustic and flavorful, this is sure to be a crowd pleaser. Be sure to serve this with bread, because your family will want to soak up every last bit of sauce!

Prep Time: 20 mins
Cook Time: 3 to 4 hrs high
6 to 8 hrs low

4 to 6 Servings

- 6 bone-in, skinless chicken thighs
- Salt and pepper, to taste
- 1 onion, diced
- Minced garlic, to taste
- 1 green bell pepper, cut into strips
- 8 ounces sliced mushrooms
- 1 can (14 ounces) diced tomatoes
- 1 can (6 ounces) tomato paste
- ½ cup chicken broth
- 1 tablespoon Italian seasoning
- 1 bay leaf (or 2 if they're smaller)
- Chopped Italian parsley, for serving (optional)
- Cooked pasta or crusty bread, your preference

1 Most bone-in thighs you're going to buy will come with the skin on them, so you'll need to remove that before you begin. If you're not comfortable with that, simply buy boneless, skinless thighs instead. This cacciatore will be just as delicious, I promise.

2 Salt and pepper the chicken and place in the slow cooker in a single layer.

3 Add the onion, garlic, bell pepper and mushrooms over the chicken.

4 In a separate bowl, mix together the tomatoes, tomato paste, chicken broth, and Italian seasoning.

5 Pour the mixture over everything in the slow cooker and top with the bay leaf.

6 Cover and cook for 3 to 4 hours on high, or on low for 6 to 8 hours.

7 Remove the bay leaf and garnish with fresh chopped parsley, if you like. Serve over pasta of your choice, or simply in a bowl with a side of bread.

Beef and Broccoli

Prep Time: 15 mins
Cook Time: 2 to 3 hrs high
4 to 6 hrs low

4 to 6 Servings

- 2 pounds flank steak, thinly sliced (or thin pre-sliced steak)
- 2 cups broccoli florets
- Salt and pepper, to taste
- ½ cup soy sauce
- ½ cup brown sugar, packed
- Minced garlic, to taste
- 1 teaspoon ground ginger
- Red pepper flakes, to taste
- Cornstarch slurry (2 tablespoons of cornstarch with 2 tablespoons of water, mixed)
- Cooked rice

1   Place the flank steak and the broccoli in the slow cooker and salt and pepper it, stirring to combine. Keep in mind that you'll be pouring the soy sauce mixture over it, so you may not want to salt and pepper as heavily as you normally would.

2   In a separate bowl, whisk together the soy sauce, brown sugar, garlic, ginger, and pepper flakes.

3   Pour the soy sauce mixture over the beef and broccoli, and stir to make sure everything is coated.

4   Cook on high for 2 to 3 hours, or low for 4 to 6 hours, stirring occasionally.

5   During the last half hour of cooking, stir in the cornstarch slurry to thicken the sauce (you'll need to turn the heat to high for this step, if you haven't already).

6   Serve over cooked rice and garnish with sesame seeds and sliced green onions.

Pork and Cauliflower Curry

Prep Time: 15 mins
Cook Time: 3 to 4 hrs high
6 to 8 hrs low

2 to 4 Servings

- 1 pound pork loin, cut into bite-size pieces
- 1 head cauliflower, cut into florets
- 1 onion, diced
- 1 can (14 ounces) diced tomatoes
- 1 can (14 ounces) coconut milk
- Minced garlic, to taste
- 2 tablespoons curry powder
- 1 teaspoon ground cumin
- 1 teaspoon ground coriander
- ½ teaspoon turmeric
- ½ teaspoon ground ginger
- Salt and pepper, to taste
- Cooked rice or naan

1. Place the pork, cauliflower, and onion in the slow cooker.

2. Mix together the tomatoes, coconut milk, garlic, curry, cumin, coriander, turmeric, ginger, and salt and pepper. Pour this mixture over everything in the slow cooker, making sure it's all well coated.

3. Cover and cook for 3 to 4 hours on high, or 6 to 8 hours on low.

4. Serve over rice or with naan.

Quick Tip: If you want a spicier curry, consider adding chili powder, cayenne, or crushed red pepper to the coconut milk mixture.

Beef Chili

Prep Time: 15 mins
Cook Time: 3 to 4 hrs high
6 to 8 hrs low

4 to 6 Servings

- 2 pounds lean ground beef
- 1 onion, diced
- 1 jalapeno, de-seeded and diced
- 1 bell pepper, diced (any color)
- 1 can (15 ounces) kidney beans, drained and rinsed
- 1 can (15 ounces) black beans, drained and rinsed
- 1 cup beef broth
- Minced garlic, to taste
- 1 can (14 ounces) diced tomatoes
- 1 can (6 ounces) tomato paste
- 2 tablespoons chili powder
- 1 teaspoon ground cumin
- 1 teaspoon smoked paprika
- ½ teaspoon dried oregano
- Salt and pepper, to taste

1 Place the ground beef in the slow cooker and spread into an even layer.

2 Add the onion, jalapeno, bell pepper, kidney beans, and black beans on top of the ground beef.

3 In a separate dish, mix together the broth, garlic, diced tomatoes, tomato paste, chili powder, cumin, paprika, oregano, salt, and pepper. Pour this over everything in the slow cooker. Don't worry about stirring into the meat right now.

4 Cover and cook for 3 to 4 hours on high, or 6 to 8 hours on low. Halfway through cooking, use a meat chopper, large spoon, or potato masher to break up the meat and combine with the other ingredients. Stir occasionally for the remainder of the cook time.

5 Serve with your choice of toppings!

Sheet Pan Dinners

These are so versatile and easy to customize to your own taste. The method is pretty much the same for all these recipes: build flavor with marinades and sauces, cook in high heat, finish under the broiler, and there's dinner!

Play around with the seasonings, and use vegetables that you enjoy to create your own versions of these sheet pan dinners. Prep the ingredients and make the marinade ahead of time, store in the fridge, and it's ready to throw onto a pan when you get home that evening.

Shrimp and Veggie Stir-Fry

 Prep Time: 20 mins
Cook Time: 12 to 15 mins

 4 Servings

- 1 pound large shrimp, peeled and deveined
- 1 red bell pepper, cut into strips
- 1 orange bell pepper, cut into strips
- 1 yellow bell pepper, cut into strips
- 1 zucchini, sliced
- 1 cup snap peas, trimmed
- 1 cup broccoli florets
- 2 tablespoons vegetable oil
- Salt and pepper, to taste
- Minced garlic, to taste
- 2 tablespoons soy sauce
- 2 tablespoons oyster sauce
- 1 tablespoon sesame oil
- 1 tablespoon honey
- 2 teaspoons ground ginger
- Cooked rice or noodles

1 Preheat the oven to 425 degrees and line a sheet pan with aluminum foil. Lightly spray with cooking spray.

2 In a bowl, mix the vegetables, shrimp, olive oil, salt and pepper to coat everything.

3 Whisk together the garlic, soy sauce, oyster sauce, sesame oil, honey and ginger, then pour over the vegetables, tossing together.

4 Pour onto the sheet pan and spread into a single layer. Use a spatula to scrape out all the remaining sauce onto the vegetables and shrimp.

5 Bake in the oven for 12 to 15 minutes, until the shrimp are pink and opaque.

6 Serve over rice or noodles, or mixed with them (I use ramen noodles and they're perfect!).

BBQ Chicken with Corn on the Cob

 Prep Time: 15 mins
Cook Time: 35 to 40 mins

 4 Servings

- 4 bone-in, skin-on chicken thighs
- 1 tablespoon baking powder
- 1 teaspoon garlic powder
- 1 teaspoon smoked paprika
- Salt and pepper, to taste
- 1 tablespoon olive oil
- 2 medium sweet potatoes, peeled and cut into bite-size pieces
- 4 ears of corn, halved
- ¼ cup barbecue sauce

1 Preheat the oven to 425 degrees. Line a sheet pan with aluminum foil and lightly spray with cooking spray.

2 Pat the chicken thighs dry with a paper towel, then toss in a bowl with the baking powder, garlic powder, paprika, and salt and pepper. Use your hands and make sure they are well coated. Lay them skin side up on the sheet pan.

3 Toss together the potatoes, olive oil, salt and pepper. Lay these in a single layer on the sheet pan.

4 Add the corn to the sheet pan.

5 Cook for 25 minutes, stirring the potatoes and flipping the corn over halfway through.

6 After 25 minutes, remove the pan from the oven and stir the vegetables again. Brush the top of the chicken (and the corn and potatoes if you want to) with the barbecue sauce and return to the oven. Cook for another 10 to 15 minutes, until the chicken is done, the barbecue sauce is thickened, and the potatoes are tender.

Quick Tip: During the last few minutes of cooking, turn the broiler to high and move the pan to the top rack to help brown and crisp the top of the chicken thighs.

Lemon Dijon Salmon and Veggies

 Prep Time: 15 mins
Cook Time: 30 mins

 4 Servings

- 4 salmon filets
- 4 tablespoons Dijon mustard
- 3 tablespoons olive oil
- Juice of 1 lemon
- 1 tablespoon garlic powder
- 1 tablespoon dried thyme
- 1 tablespoon dried rosemary
- Salt and pepper, to taste
- 1 pound baby potatoes, halved
- 1 bunch of asparagus, trimmed

1 Preheat the oven to 400 degrees and line a sheet pan with aluminum foil. Lightly spray with cooking spray.

2 Brush or spread the mustard over the tops of the salmon filets. Season with salt and pepper and a bit of the rosemary and thyme if you prefer. Set aside.

3 In a small bowl, whisk together the olive oil, lemon juice, and seasonings.

4 Place the potatoes on the sheet pan and drizzle half the olive oil mixture over them, tossing to fully coat. Arrange the potatoes in a single layer and bake in the oven for 15 minutes.

5 While the potatoes are cooking, toss the asparagus with the remainder of the olive oil mixture.

6 After 15 minutes, remove the pan from the oven and move the potatoes to one side. Add the asparagus and salmon to the pan and return to the oven. Bake for another 15 minutes, or until the salmon is cooked through. It should flake apart easily with a fork.

7 Serve it hot, with a bit of lemon squeezed over, and fresh chopped parsley if you're feeling cute.

Quick Tip: If you prefer, for the last 3 to 4 minutes of cooking, you can turn the broiler on and move the pan to the top rack to add some color to the salmon and crisp up the potatoes a bit. If you do this, keep a close eye on it.

Italian Chicken with Zesty Veggies

 Prep Time: 15 mins
Cook Time: 20 to 25 mins

 4 Servings

- 4 boneless, skinless chicken breasts
- Your favorite Italian dressing
- 3 tablespoons butter, melted
- 2 tablespoons olive oil
- Juice of 1 lemon
- 1 packet zesty Italian seasoning mix
- 1 pound baby potatoes, halved (or cut into bite-size pieces)
- 1 pound fresh green beans, trimmed
- Salt and pepper, to taste

1. Preheat the oven to 400 degrees. Line a sheet pan with aluminum foil and lightly spray with cooking spray.

2. In a bag or airtight container, add the chicken breasts with a generous amount of Italian dressing, making sure the chicken is entirely coated. Set aside. If you can do this a couple hours beforehand and leave them in the fridge, even better.

3. In a bowl, whisk together the butter, olive oil, lemon juice and Italian seasoning mix.

4. Toss the potatoes and green beans in the butter mixture and spread in an even layer on one side of the sheet pan. Drizzle any remaining mixture over the top.

5. On the other side of the sheet pan, arrange the chicken breasts in a single layer.

6. Salt and pepper everything on the sheet pan.

7. Bake for 20 to 25 minutes, until the chicken is cooked through and the potatoes are tender.

8. Let the chicken rest for a few minutes, then slice and serve with the potatoes and green beans.

Quick Tip: Just before removing from the oven, turn the broiler on to high heat and place the sheet pan on the top rack. Keep a close eye on it, and let it broil for about 3 minutes, long enough to brown the chicken and potatoes.

Chicken Veggie Bake

 Prep Time: 15 mins
Cook Time: 30 mins

 4 Servings

- Juice of 1 lemon
- 3 tablespoons olive oil
- 1 teaspoon garlic powder
- Salt and pepper, to taste
- 1 tablespoon Italian seasoning
- 4 boneless, skinless chicken breasts
- 1 pint cherry tomatoes, halved
- 1 red bell pepper, sliced
- 1 yellow bell pepper, sliced
- 1 red onion, sliced
- 1 zucchini, sliced
- 1 yellow squash, sliced
- Crumbled feta cheese
- Balsamic glaze, for serving

1 Preheat the oven to 400 degrees. Line a sheet pan with aluminum foil and lightly spray with cooking spray.

2 Whisk together the olive oil, lemon juice, salt, pepper, Italian seasoning, and garlic powder.

3 Arrange the chicken and vegetables in an even layer on the baking sheet. Drizzle the lemon juice mixture over everything, tossing to coat evenly. Use your hands to ensure the chicken is fully coated.

4 Bake for 30 minutes, flipping the chicken and stirring the vegetables halfway through.

5 Once the chicken is cooked through, allow to stand for a few minutes, then slice and serve with the vegetables. Sprinkle a few handfuls of feta cheese over everything. Drizzle with balsamic glaze or any other sauce you prefer.

Pork and Pineapple Skewers

Prep Time: 15 mins
Cook Time: 25 mins

4 Servings

- ¼ cup soy sauce
- 2 tablespoons honey
- 2 tablespoons olive oil
- Minced garlic, to taste
- 1 teaspoon ground ginger
- Salt and pepper, to taste
- Red pepper flakes, to taste (optional)
- 1 pound pork tenderloin, cut into cubes
- 1 can pineapple chunks
- 1 red bell pepper, cut into chunks
- 1 green bell pepper, cut into chunks
- 1 red onion, cut into chunks
- Cooked rice
- Sesame seeds, for serving
- Sliced green onions, for serving

1. Preheat the oven to 400 degrees. Line a sheet pan with aluminum foil and lightly spray with cooking spray.
2. Whisk together the soy sauce, honey, olive oil, garlic, ginger, salt and pepper, and red pepper flakes.
3. Place the pork, pineapple chunks, bell pepper and onion onto the skewers, alternating ingredients. If using wooden skewers, soak them in water for half an hour prior to cooking to prevent burning.
4. Drizzle or brush the soy sauce marinade over the skewers, coating everything evenly (reserve a little marinade for step 6).
5. Lay the skewers on the sheet pan and cook for 25 minutes, until the pork is done, flipping halfway through.
6. During the last few minutes of cooking, turn the broiler to high. Drizzle the reserved marinade over the skewers and move them to the top rack for a few minutes. Keep a close eye on them until the broiler browns them a bit.
7. Serve hot over rice, garnished with sesame seeds and sliced green onions.

Shrimp Boil

 Prep Time: 15 mins
Cook Time: 30 to 45 mins

 4 Servings

- Juice of 2 lemons
- 2 tablespoons olive oil
- 2 tablespoons Old Bay seasoning
- 1 tablespoon Cajun seasoning of your choice
- 1 tablespoon liquid crab boil, if available (if you don't have any, it's not a dealbreaker)
- Salt, to taste
- 1 pound baby red potatoes, cut into bite-size pieces
- 4 ears of corn, cut in halves
- 1 pound smoked sausage or Andouille sausage, sliced into rounds
- 1 onion, cut into chunks
- 1 pound large shrimp, peeled and deveined

1. Preheat the oven to 400 degrees. Line a sheet pan with aluminum foil and lightly spray with cooking spray.

2. Mix together the lemon juice, olive oil, Old Bay, Cajun seasoning, and crab boil. Add salt at your discretion. Check the label on the Cajun seasoning you use, some have more salt than others. Reserve about ¼ of this mixture to the side.

3. Toss the potatoes, corn, sausage and onion in the mixture, making sure everything is well coated.

4. Arrange everything in an even layer on the baking sheet. Cook for 25 to 35 minutes, or until potatoes are almost done.

5. While the sausage and vegetables are cooking, toss the shrimp in the reserved lemon juice marinade. Use the same bowl you just used for everything else.

6. Remove the pan, give everything a stir and flip the corn cobs over. Add the shrimp to the pan and return to the oven for another 8 to 10 minutes, until the shrimp are cooked through and opaque.

7. Serve hot with any sauces or accompaniments you enjoy!

Quick Tip: Feel free to play around with the ratios of the marinade ingredients. If you think you'd prefer more Cajun seasoning than Old Bay, or extra crab boil, go for it!

Beef Fajitas

 Prep Time: 20 mins
Cook Time: 15 mins

 4 to 6 Servings

- 2 tablespoons olive oil
- Juice of 1 lime
- 1 packet fajita seasoning
- Salt and pepper, to taste
- 1 pound flank steak, thinly sliced
- 1 red bell pepper, thinly sliced
- 1 green bell pepper, thinly sliced
- 1 yellow bell pepper, thinly sliced
- 1 onion, thinly sliced
- Flour tortillas

1 Preheat the oven to 400 degrees. Line a sheet pan with aluminum foil and lightly spray with cooking spray.

2 In a large bowl, whisk together the olive oil, lime juice, fajita seasoning, and salt and pepper.

3 Add the steak and vegetables to the bowl and mix to combine everything.

4 Arrange everything in an even layer on the baking sheet and cook for 15 minutes.

5 While the meat and vegetables are cooking, warm the tortillas.

6 Serve hot with your favorite toppings.

Parmesan Ranch Pork Chops

 Prep Time: 15 mins
Cook Time: 20 to 25 mins

 4 Servings

- ¾ cup mayonnaise
- ¼ cup grated Parmesan cheese
- 1 packet ranch seasoning mix
- 4 boneless pork chops
- Salt and pepper, to taste
- Cornbread stuffing mix
- 1 pound Brussels sprouts, trimmed and halved

1. Preheat the oven to 400 degrees. Line a sheet pan with aluminum foil and lightly spray with cooking spray.

2. In a bowl, mix together the mayonnaise, Parmesan cheese, and ranch seasoning.

3. Arrange the pork chops in a single layer on the sheet pan, and salt and pepper them (easy on the salt, because you're about to add ranch and Parmesan cheese). Spread a spoonful of the mayo mixture across the top of each one. Sprinkle an even layer of the dry cornbread stuffing over each chop, and lightly spray with cooking spray so the top browns in the oven.

4. Add the Brussels sprouts to the bowl with the mayo mixture, salt and pepper, and ¼ cup of the cornbread stuffing. Mix to combine and make sure all the sprouts are coated. Spread these in an even layer on the other side of the sheet pan.

5. Cook for 20 to 25 minutes, or until the chops are cooked through. The tops should brown on their own, but if you want to crisp them up a bit more, turn the broiler on and move the pan to the top rack for the last couple minutes.

Quick Tip: If you'd like a starch to go with this, make a little extra mayo mixture and toss it with a pound of potatoes cut into bite-size pieces and add to the sheet pan. If you like your Brussels sprouts more tender, pop them in the oven for 10 to 15 minutes before adding the pork chops to the pan.

Coconut Lime Shrimp and Quinoa

 Prep Time: 10 mins
Cook Time: 15 mins

 2 to 4 Servings

FOR THE SHEET PAN:

- 2 tablespoons coconut oil, melted
- Juice of 1 lime
- 1 teaspoon red pepper flakes
- 1 teaspoon ground ginger
- Salt and pepper, to taste
- 1 pound large shrimp, peeled and deveined
- 1 red bell pepper, sliced or cut into chunks
- 1 can (20 ounces) pineapple chunks, drained

FOR THE QUINOA:

- 2 cups vegetable stock
- 1 cup quinoa
- Juice of 1 lime
- Handful of cilantro, chopped

1 Preheat the oven to 400 degrees. Line a sheet pan with aluminum foil and lightly spray with cooking spray.

2 In a large bowl, whisk together the coconut oil, lime juice, red pepper flakes, ground ginger, and salt and pepper.

3 Add the shrimp, bell pepper and pineapple chunks. Toss with the coconut mixture to make sure everything is coated.

4 Arrange on the sheet pan in an even layer. Drizzle any remaining marinade over the top.

5 Cook for 10 to 12 minutes, until the shrimp is cooked through and opaque.

6 Add the vegetable stock and quinoa to a saucepan over medium high heat.

7 Bring to a boil, then reduce to simmer and cover. Cook for 15 minutes, until most of the liquid is absorbed.

8 Remove from the heat and uncover, allowing it to stand for a few minutes.

9 Fluff with a fork and stir in the lime juice and cilantro.

Chipotle Lime Chicken Drumsticks

Prep Time: 15 mins
Cook Time: 35 mins

3 to 4 Servings

- 2 tablespoons olive oil
- 2 tablespoons chipotle peppers in adobo sauce, minced
- Juice of 2 limes
- 1 teaspoon garlic powder
- 1 teaspoon ground cumin
- 1 teaspoon paprika
- Salt and pepper, to taste
- One 12-ounce bag frozen corn kernels
- 12 ounces fresh green beans, trimmed
- 6 chicken drumsticks

1   Preheat the oven to 400 degrees. Line a sheet pan with aluminum foil and lightly spray with cooking spray.

2   Whisk together the olive oil, peppers, lime juice, garlic powder, cumin, paprika, and salt and pepper.

3   Toss the vegetables with half the marinade and arrange on one side of the sheet pan in a single layer.

4   Toss the drumsticks with the rest of the marinade and arrange in a single layer on the other side of the pan.

5   Bake for 30 minutes, until the chicken is cooked through. Turn the drumsticks over and stir the vegetables halfway through.

6   Move to the top rack and broil on high for 3 to 5 minutes to brown the chicken.

Maple Dijon Glazed Chicken

Prep Time: 15 mins
Cook Time: 35 to 40 mins

4 Servings

- 4 bone-in, skin-on chicken thighs
- 1 tablespoon baking powder
- Salt and pepper, to taste
- ¼ cup maple syrup
- 2 tablespoons Dijon mustard
- 1 tablespoon honey
- 1 tablespoon olive oil
- 1 teaspoon garlic powder
- 1 teaspoon dried thyme
- Salt and pepper, to taste
- 1 pound Brussels sprouts, trimmed and halved
- 2 medium sweet potatoes, peeled and cut into bite-size pieces

1 Preheat the oven to 425 degrees. Line a sheet pan with aluminum foil and lightly spray with cooking spray.

2 Pat the chicken thighs dry with a paper towel, then toss in a bowl with the baking powder, salt, and pepper. Use your hands and make sure they are well coated. Lay them skin side up on the sheet pan.

3 In a small bowl, whisk together the syrup, mustard, honey, olive oil, garlic powder, thyme, salt, and pepper. Reserve a couple tablespoons to the side.

4 Toss the Brussels sprouts and sweet potatoes in the maple marinade, and then lay them out on the sheet pan in an even layer.

5 Cook for 25 minutes, stirring the vegetables halfway through.

6 After 25 minutes, brush the remaining maple marinade over the chicken thighs and stir the vegetables again. Return to the oven and cook another 10 to 15 minutes, until the chicken is done, and the potatoes are tender.

7 Move to the top rack and broil on high for 3 to 5 minutes to brown the chicken.

Sausage and Gnocchi

Prep Time: 10 mins
Cook Time: 25 to 35 mins

4 Servings

- 5 tablespoons olive oil
- Juice of 2 lemons
- Salt and pepper, to taste
- 2 packets of zesty Italian seasoning mix
- 1 pound cherry tomatoes
- 12 to 16 ounces broccoli florets
- 1 red bell pepper, cut into chunks
- ½ large red onion, or 1 small one, cut into chunks
- 1 pound smoked Cajun sausage (or your choice of sausage)
- 1 pound gnocchi
- Feta cheese, crumbled, about 1 cup

1. Preheat the oven to 425 degrees. Line a sheet pan with aluminum foil and lightly spray with cooking spray.
2. Whisk together the olive oil, lemon juice, salt, pepper, and Italian seasoning mix.
3. In a large bowl, toss together the vegetables and a little more than half the marinade.
4. Cut the sausage into rounds about ¼ inch thick, or however thick you like. This part really isn't important, it's personal preference.
5. Spread the vegetables out on the sheet pan with the sausage.
6. Bake for 15 minutes. While that's cooking, open up the gnocchi and toss with the remaining marinade.
7. Remove the sheet pan from the oven, stir the vegetables, and sprinkle the gnocchi over the top. Drizzle any remaining marinade over the pan.
8. Return to the oven and cook for another 10 to 15 minutes, until the gnocchi is done. It should have a toasty, fluffy texture.
9. Turn on the broiler and move the pan to the top rack for 3 to 5 minutes. This should help toast the gnocchi, blister the tomatoes, and brown the sausage a bit more.
10. Remove from the oven and sprinkle the feta cheese over the top and serve. This is how I like mine, but if you'd prefer to add the cheese before putting the pan under the broiler, that would be delicious too!

Spicy Peanut Chicken

 Prep Time: 15 mins
Cook Time: 20 mins

 4 Servings

- ½ cup peanut butter
- ½ cup soy sauce
- ½ cup warm water
- 2 tablespoons sesame oil
- 2 tablespoons honey
- 2 tablespoons rice vinegar
- 1 tablespoon + 1 teaspoon Sriracha
- 1 teaspoon garlic powder
- 1 teaspoon ground ginger
- 1 teaspoon red pepper flakes
- Juice of 2 limes
- 3 boneless, skinless chicken breasts, cut into chunks
- 1 pound broccoli florets
- Rice, for serving (I prefer Jasmine)

1 Preheat the oven to 400 degrees. Line a sheet pan with aluminum foil and lightly spray with cooking spray.

2 Whisk together all the ingredients for the sauce.

3 In a large bowl, toss together the chicken, broccoli, and about half the sauce.

4 Spread everything out in an even layer on the sheet pan and bake for 15 minutes.

5 Remove from the oven, stir, drizzle a bit more sauce over the top, and place under the broiler on high for 3 to 5 minutes, until the broccoli starts to char, the sauce thickens, and the chicken browns.

6 Serve hot over the rice, with more sauce.

Quick Tip: This recipe will make more than enough sauce, so feel free to cut it in half if you want. I enjoy lots of sauce over my rice, so I make extra.

Cajun Ranch Chicken Breasts

Prep Time: 15 mins
Cook Time: 25 mins

4 Servings

- 2 to 3 tablespoons olive oil
- 2 tablespoons ranch seasoning mix
- 2 tablespoons Cajun seasoning of your choice
- One 12-ounce bag of frozen corn kernels
- 1 pound okra, trimmed and halved lengthwise
- 4 boneless, skinless chicken breasts

1   Preheat the oven to 400 degrees. Line a sheet pan with aluminum foil and lightly spray with cooking spray.

2   In a bowl, toss together the vegetables with just enough olive oil to coat them. Add half the seasonings and mix well to coat the vegetables entirely.

3   Place the vegetables on one side of the sheet pan, in a single layer.

4   Add the chicken breasts to the bowl, with just enough vegetable oil to coat them. Add the other half of the seasonings and mix to coat the chicken.

5   Place the chicken on the other half of the sheet pan in a single layer.

6   Bake for 25 minutes, stirring the corn and okra halfway through.

Quick Tip: Depending on how much salt is in the Cajun seasoning you use, you may need to add a bit.

Honey Dijon Drumsticks

Prep Time: 10 mins
Cook Time: 55 mins

3 to 4 Servings

- 4 tablespoons olive oil
- ¼ cup honey
- 2 tablespoons Dijon mustard
- 1 teaspoon garlic powder
- 1 tablespoon apple cider vinegar
- 1 teaspoon paprika
- Salt and pepper, to taste
- 1 pound baby carrots
- 1 head cauliflower, cut into florets
- 6 chicken drumsticks

1 Preheat the oven to 400 degrees. Line a sheet pan with aluminum foil and lightly spray with cooking spray.

2 Whisk together all the ingredients for the sauce.

3 In a bowl, toss together the carrots with enough sauce to coat them.

4 Lay the carrots in a single layer on the sheet pan and bake for 20 minutes.

5 While the carrots bake, toss the cauliflower with enough sauce to coat them.

6 Once the carrots have baked for 20 minutes, move them over to one side of the pan and add the cauliflower.

7 Toss the drumsticks with the remaining sauce and arrange them in a single layer on the pan.

8 Return to the oven and cook for another 30 minutes, until the chicken is cooked through. Stir the vegetables halfway through.

9 Move the pan to the top rack under the broiler on high for 3 to 5 minutes, to brown the drumsticks.

One-Pot Meals

There was one requirement for a recipe to make it into this section of the book: it had to use only one pot on the stove.

These are simple, tasty meals that I love and hope you will too. Like the slow cooker recipes, feel free to mix up and change out ingredients to make the dish your own. You'll notice that each starch tends to follow the same basic format. Once you get the hang of cooking one-pot meals, you can begin to create your own recipes, using flavors you enjoy.

Chorizo Chicken Skillet

 Prep Time: 10 mins
Cook Time: 35 to 45 mins

 4 Servings

- 9 ounces chorizo
- 1 onion, diced
- Minced garlic, to taste
- 2 large chicken breasts, cut into bite-size pieces
- 3 ounces tomato paste
- 1½ cups long grain rice
- Salt and pepper, to taste
- 1 teaspoon smoked paprika
- 1 teaspoon your favorite Cajun seasoning
- 3 cups chicken stock
- 1 cup shredded cheese of your preference (I prefer Monterey Jack or Colby Jack)

1. In a wide pan over medium high heat, sauté the onion and chorizo together for 5 to 10 minutes, until the onion begins to soften.
2. In a separate bowl, mix together the chicken and all seasonings, until well coated.
3. Once the chorizo and onions are ready, add the garlic and sauté for an additional 30 seconds to a minute, until fragrant.
4. Add the chicken to the pan. Brown it for approximately 5 minutes, stirring occasionally. You don't need to cook the chicken all the way through, just get a little color on it.
5. Now stir in the tomato paste, allowing it to cook for a couple minutes and begin to caramelize.
6. Add the rice, stirring together until all rice is thoroughly coated.
7. Pour in the chicken stock. Reduce to a simmer and cover, cooking for 20 minutes. Uncover, stir, and simmer uncovered for another 5 to 10 minutes, until the liquid is absorbed and the rice is fully cooked.
8. Cut the heat off but leave the pan on the burner. Sprinkle an even layer of cheese over the top and return the lid. Let it sit for another 5 minutes, until the cheese is melted.
9. Serve and enjoy!

Kinda Sorta Chicken Alfredo

 Prep Time: 10 mins
Cook Time: 30 mins

 4 Servings

- 4 to 5 thin-sliced chicken breasts
- Salt and pepper, to taste
- Paprika, to taste
- 2 tablespoons olive oil
- Minced garlic, to taste
- 1½ cups chicken stock
- 1½ cups heavy cream
- Red pepper flakes, to taste
- 1 teaspoon each garlic powder and onion powder
- 2 teaspoons Italian seasoning
- 8 ounces fettuccine pasta
- One 12-ounce package frozen, steamable broccoli florets
- 5 ounces soft cheese of your choice (e.g., goat cheese, Boursin, Alouette)

1 Season the chicken breasts on both sides generously with the salt, pepper, and paprika.

2 In a preheated wide pan over medium-high heat, add the oil and when shimmering, sauté the chicken until browned and cooked through (thinly sliced breasts should only take 3 to 5 minutes each side, reaching 165 degrees internal).

3 Remove the chicken to a separate plate and set aside.

4 Turn the heat to medium-low, and add the garlic to the pan, cooking for about a minute, until fragrant. Add the chicken stock, cream, and seasonings. Stir together and cook until it comes back to a simmer.

5 Turn the heat down to a low simmer, and add the fettuccine. Cover and cook for 10 to 12 minutes, stirring occasionally, until the pasta is done.

6 While the pasta is cooking, steam the broccoli in the microwave, following the package instructions.

7 When the pasta is done, add the cheese and stir until fully melted and combined. Stir in the broccoli.

8 Slice the chicken breasts on a bias, against the grain, and serve over the pasta.

Quick Tip: If you'd rather have the chicken mixed in with the pasta, cut the chicken into bite-size pieces. Sauté according to the instructions above, and simply leave them in the pan and cook with the pasta.

Broccoli Cheese Orzo

 Prep Time: 10 mins
Cook Time: 30 mins

 4 Servings

- 2 tablespoons butter
- 1 onion, diced
- 4 ounces matchstick carrots
- Salt and pepper, to taste
- Minced garlic, to taste
- 8 ounces orzo pasta
- 2 cups chicken stock
- 1 cup heavy cream
- One 12-ounce microwaveable bag frozen broccoli florets
- 4 ounces shredded cheddar cheese
- Shredded rotisserie chicken (optional)

1. In a wide pan over medium high heat, sauté the onion and butter until they begin to soften, about 5 minutes.
2. Add the carrots, salt, and pepper. Stir together and continue cooking until the vegetables are soft, another 5 to 10 minutes.
3. Add the garlic to the pan and cook until fragrant, about a minute.
4. Pour the pasta into the pan and stir with the vegetables, and toast for about a minute.
5. Add the chicken stock and heavy cream.
6. Bring to a simmer, then cover and cook for 12 minutes, stirring occasionally. If the pasta begins to get too dry, add a splash more stock, water, or cream. This should have a loose, creamy consistency.
7. While the orzo is simmering, prepare the broccoli according to the package instructions.
8. When the orzo is done, add the broccoli and the cheese to the pan and stir together until smooth. Season with more salt and pepper as needed.
9. Add rotisserie chicken if desired. Stir the chicken in after everything else is complete.

Sun-Dried Tomato Chicken

 Prep Time: 10 mins
Cook Time: 30 mins

 4 Servings

- 4 to 5 thin-sliced chicken breasts
- Salt and pepper, to taste
- Paprika, to taste
- 2 tablespoons olive oil
- Minced garlic, to taste
- 1 cup sun-dried tomatoes, chopped
- 2 cups chicken stock
- 1 teaspoon Italian seasoning
- 8 ounces penne pasta (or any pasta you prefer)
- ½ cup heavy cream
- ¼ cup grated Parmesan cheese
- 2 large handfuls of fresh baby spinach

1. Season the chicken breasts on both sides generously with the salt, pepper, and paprika.
2. In a preheated wide pan over medium-high heat, add the oil and when shimmering, sauté the chicken until browned and cooked through (thin-sliced breasts should only take 3 to 5 minutes each side, reaching 165 degrees internal).
3. Remove the chicken to a separate plate and set aside.
4. Sauté the garlic and tomatoes together until fragrant, about a minute or two.
5. Add the chicken stock and Italian seasoning, stirring to combine with the tomatoes and garlic. Once boiling, add the pasta, reduce to a simmer, and cover. Cook for about 12 minutes until the pasta is done.
6. Once the pasta is finished, stir in the heavy cream and once it's fully incorporated and heated through, add the Parmesan cheese. Stir until the cheese is melted and smooth.
7. Add the spinach and cover. Let it stand for a few minutes until the spinach begins to soften and wilt, 3 to 5 minutes. Mix the spinach into the pasta until it's fully wilted.
8. Slice the chicken breasts on a bias, against the grain, and serve over the pasta.

Quick Tip: If you'd rather have the chicken mixed in with the pasta, cut the chicken into bite-size pieces. Sauté according to the instructions above, and simply leave them in the pan and cook with the pasta.

Pork Rice

 Prep Time: 10 mins
Cook Time: 40 mins

 4 to 6 Servings

- 1 pound ground pork
- Minced garlic, to taste
- 1 bag of frozen stir-fry vegetables
- Salt and pepper, to taste
- ¼ cup soy sauce
- 2 tablespoons oyster sauce
- 1 tablespoon sesame oil
- 1 tablespoon brown sugar
- 1 teaspoon ground ginger
- 1 cup rice
- 2 cups beef stock

1 In a wide pan over medium high heat, brown the ground pork. Drain any grease if necessary.

2 Stir the garlic into the pork and sauté until fragrant, about a minute. Mix in the frozen vegetables and add salt and pepper (remember you're about to add sauce to this, so be conservative). Cook over medium high heat for another 3 to 5 minutes, until the vegetables thaw and begin to soften.

3 In a separate bowl, whisk together the soy sauce, oyster sauce, sesame oil, brown sugar, and ginger.

4 Pour the sauce mixture over the pork and vegetables and stir to coat everything. Add the rice and mix until all the rice is coated in the sauce.

5 Add the beef stock, bring to a boil, then reduce the heat to a simmer and cover. Cook for 20 to 25 minutes until the rice is cooked through, stirring occasionally.

6 Once the rice is done, remove from the heat and let it stand, covered, for a few minutes to steam.

7 Serve with sliced green onions and sesame seeds. I drizzle mine with a bit of yum-yum sauce.

Breakfast Skillet

 Prep Time: 5 mins
Cook Time: 20 mins

 4 to 6 Servings

- 1 pound chorizo
- 1 pound frozen breakfast potatoes with peppers and onions
- 6 eggs
- Salt and pepper
- 4 ounces shredded cheese of your choice, (optional)
- Minced chives and/or sliced green onions, for serving

1 In a wide pan over medium high heat, brown the chorizo. Soak up a little of the excess grease with a paper towel, but leave some to cook the potatoes in.

2 Add the potatoes, stir well into the chorizo, and cook for about 10 minutes, stirring occasionally, until the potatoes are fork tender.

3 Turn the heat to simmer, and gently crack the eggs over the potatoes and chorizo.

4 Salt and pepper the eggs to taste, cover, and cook until the eggs are done to your liking.

5 Add the shredded cheese prior to cracking the eggs, or save it for garnish on top (if using).

6 Add chives, green onions, more cheese, or anything you like!

Beef and Rice

Prep Time: 10 mins
Cook Time: 35 mins

4 to 6 Servings

- 1 pound ground beef
- 1 onion, diced
- 1 green bell pepper, diced
- 1 can (14.5 ounces) corn, drained
- 1 can (14.5 ounces) black beans, drained and rinsed
- 1 can (14.5 ounces) diced tomatoes, not drained
- 1 packet of taco seasoning
- 1 cup rice
- 2 cups beef stock

1   In a wide pan over medium high heat, brown the ground beef. Drain any grease if necessary.

2   Add the onion and bell pepper and cook until they begin to soften, about 5 minutes.

3   Stir in the corn, beans, tomatoes, taco seasoning, rice and beef stock. Bring to a boil, then reduce the heat to a simmer and cover. Cook for 20 to 25 minutes, stirring occasionally, until the rice is done.

4   Once the rice is cooked through, remove from the heat and let stand uncovered for another 5 minutes, until it thickens.

5   Serve with your favorite toppings (shredded cheese, sour cream, cilantro, etc.) and enjoy!

Onion Butter Steak and Potatoes

Prep Time: 10 mins
Cook Time: 20 mins

4 Servings

- 1 pound sirloin (or steak of your choice) cut into chunks
- Salt and pepper, to taste
- 1 tablespoon olive oil
- 1 pound baby potatoes, cut into bite-size pieces
- 1 tablespoon olive oil
- 8 ounces fresh snap peas
- 3 tablespoons butter, melted
- 1 tablespoons Worcestershire sauce
- 1 packet onion soup mix

1 Salt and pepper the sirloin pieces. Heat up a wide pan over high heat. Add the olive oil and then the steak in a single layer. Do not move the steak once it's in the pan. Let it get a nice sear on one side, 2 to 3 minutes, before turning over to the other side. Once the steak is browned on two sides, remove to a plate and set aside.

2 Add the potatoes to the pan along with another tablespoon or so of olive oil, salt and pepper. Stir or toss to coat the potatoes fully. After cooking the potatoes for 2 to 3 minutes, add a small splash of water to the pan and stir. This will deglaze the pan, coating your potatoes in all that steak flavor. Reduce the heat to medium low, cover, and let the potatoes cook for 5 minutes, stirring occasionally.

3 Add the snap peas to the pan. Cover and cook for another 5 minutes, stirring occasionally.

4 Whisk together the melted butter, Worcestershire, and onion soup mix, and pour over the potatoes and snap peas. Stir to combine. At this point, you'll need to decide if you'd like your steak cooked more, or if you're happy with how it came out of the pan earlier. If you'd like to cook it a bit more, go ahead and add it to the pan now and stir in with everything else. Cover and cook for about another 5 minutes, until the potatoes are fork tender.

Goat Cheese Gnocchi and Meatball Soup

 Prep Time: 5 mins
Cook Time: 25 mins

 4 Servings

- Approximately ¾ cup sun-dried tomatoes, chopped
- 1 tablespoon of the oil the sun-dried tomatoes came packed in
- Minced garlic, to taste
- 1.5 pounds frozen meatballs of your preference
- 3 cups chicken stock
- 1 tablespoon Italian seasoning
- 1 teaspoon red pepper flakes, optional
- 1 pound gnocchi
- 4 ounces goat cheese (or grated Parmesan cheese if you prefer) + more for serving
- 2 handfuls of fresh baby spinach

1. In a wide pan over medium high heat, sauté the tomatoes, oil, and garlic until fragrant, 1 to 2 minutes.
2. If you remembered to remove the meatballs from the freezer to thaw, then add them to the pan and brown them for a couple minutes. Otherwise, see the next step.
3. Add the meatballs, chicken stock, Italian seasoning and red pepper flakes to the pan, stirring to combine. Bring to a boil, then reduce to a simmer and cover. Cook for 15 to 20 minutes, until the meatballs are fully heated through. (Less time if yours were thawed.)
4. Add the gnocchi and goat cheese. The gnocchi will only take 3 to 4 minutes to cook. By that time, you should be able to stir the cheese in until it's smooth and incorporated.
5. Add the spinach on top, and cover again. Let it sit for a few minutes until the spinach begins to wilt, then stir it in.
6. Remove from the heat and let it stand uncovered for a few minutes to thicken.
7. Top with goat cheese crumbles or Parmesan cheese and serve it up!

Italian Sausage Rigatoni

 Prep Time: 10 mins
Cook Time: 20 mins

 4 Servings

- 1 pound ground Italian sausage (mild or spicy, your choice)
- 1 onion, diced
- 1 green bell pepper, diced
- Minced garlic, to taste
- 3 tablespoons tomato paste
- 1 can (8 ounces) tomato sauce
- 2½ cups chicken stock
- 1 cup heavy cream
- 1 tablespoon Italian seasoning
- Salt and pepper, to taste
- 1 teaspoon red pepper flakes
- 8 ounces rigatoni pasta
- Grated Parmesan cheese, for serving

1. In a wide pan over medium high heat, brown the sausage. Drain any grease.

2. Add the bell pepper and onion and cook with the sausage until the vegetables begin to soften.

3. Add the garlic and cook until fragrant, 1 to 2 minutes.

4. Add the tomato paste and stir until well combined, cooking until it begins to carmelize, 3 to 5 minutes.

5. Pour in the tomato sauce, chicken stock, and cream, with the Italian seasoning, salt and pepper, and red pepper flakes.

6. Bring to a boil, then reduce to a simmer and stir in the pasta. Cover and cook for 10 to 12 minutes, until pasta is done.

7. Uncover the pasta and remove from the heat. Let stand until the sauce thickens. Top with grated Parmesan.

Taco Taters

 Prep Time: 5 mins
Cook Time: 25 mins

 4 Servings

- Splash of olive oil
- 1 pound baby potatoes, cut into bite-size pieces
- 1 packet of taco seasoning mix
- 1 pound lean ground beef
- 1 can (10 ounces) diced tomatoes with green chilies
- 4 ounces shredded cheese of your choice (optional)
- For serving: pico de gallo, avocado, and/or sour cream

1. In a wide pan over medium high heat, add enough olive oil to coat the potatoes. Add the potatoes and toss with the olive oil until well coated. Salt them and sprinkle about half the packet of taco seasoning onto them, and stir until combined. Cook for about 5 minutes, stirring occasionally.

2. Shove the potatoes over to one side of the pan, and add the ground beef. Cook the beef until done, then mix with the potatoes.

3. Add the can of tomatoes, with the juice. Add a splash of water, along with the remainder of the taco seasoning, and mix well.

4. Cover and reduce the heat to a simmer, and cook for another 10 minutes, stirring occasionally, until the potatoes are fork tender.

5. If using, add the shredded cheese over the top, cut the heat off, and cover. Let stand until the cheese is melted.

6. Service with pico de gallo, avocado, sour cream, cheese, and any other toppings that sound good to you!

Creamy Lemon Shrimp Orzo

 Prep Time: 5 mins
Cook Time: 25 mins

 4 to 6 Servings

- 1 pound large shrimp, peeled and deveined
- 1 tablespoon paprika
- 1 teaspoon garlic powder
- Salt and pepper, to taste
- 1 tablespoon olive oil
- Minced garlic, to taste
- Juice of 2 lemons
- 1 pound orzo pasta
- 3 cups chicken or vegetable stock
- ½ cup heavy cream
- 1 teaspoon dried thyme
- Grated Parmesan cheese, for serving

1 Mix together the shrimp with the paprika, garlic powder, and salt and pepper until it's fully coated.

2 In a wide pan over medium heat, heat the olive oil. Add the shrimp and sauté on each side for about 2 minutes, until the shrimp are pink and opaque. Remove and set aside.

3 Add the garlic to the pan (add a splash more olive oil if necessary) and cook until fragrant, about a minute. Add the juice from one lemon to deglaze the pan.

4 Add the orzo to the pan and sauté for 1 to 2 minutes until it begins to brown a bit. Add the juice from the other lemon and stir to combine.

5 Pour in the chicken stock, heavy cream, salt and pepper, and thyme and mix together with the orzo. Bring to a boil, then reduce to a simmer. Cover and cook for 10 to 12 minutes, until the orzo is cooked through and the liquid is absorbed.

6 Add the shrimp to the pasta and stir in. Top with grated Parmesan cheese.

Cajun Ranch Chicken Sausage Pasta

 Prep Time: 15 mins
Cook Time: 30 mins

 4 to 6 Servings

- 1 pound andouille sausage, cut into rounds
- 4 to 6 boneless, skinless chicken thighs, cut into bite-size pieces
- 1 onion, diced
- 1 red bell pepper, diced
- 2 celery ribs, diced
- Salt and pepper, to taste
- 1 tablespoon Cajun seasoning
- Minced garlic, to taste
- 8 ounces penne pasta
- 2 cups chicken stock
- 1 cup heavy cream
- 2 tablespoons ranch seasoning mix
- 8 ounces Monterey Jack cheese, shredded

1 In a wide, heavy pan or Dutch oven, brown the sausage.

2 Remove the sausage to a paper towel lined plate.

3 Add the chicken to the hot pan and brown in the sausage fat, for 3 to 5 minutes. Season with salt, pepper, and Cajun seasoning.

4 Add the onion, bell pepper, and celery and cook with the chicken until softened, another 3 to 5 minutes. Season with salt, pepper, and Cajun seasoning.

5 Add the minced garlic and cook until fragrant, about a minute.

6 Return the sausage to the pan, along with the pasta. Stir to combine everything.

7 Add the chicken stock, cream, and ranch seasoning, mixing well.

8 Bring to a boil, then reduce to a simmer and cover. Cook for 12 to 15 minutes, stirring occasionally, until the pasta is done.

9 Remove from the heat and stir in the cheese until melted.

10 Let stand for about 5 minutes so the sauce will thicken.

Rotisserie Realness

This section of the book was inspired by a series I did earlier this year, where I cooked the audience's favorite shortcut rotisserie recipes. Rotisserie chicken is a quick, easy, and usually affordable base for simple dinner options.

These recipes use just about every shortcut possible. We're trying to get dinner on the table as fast as possible, and with as little effort as we can. I used two cups of shredded rotisserie as my standard of measurement, just to put a nice round number on it. Use however much you get off a chicken or use half and save the rest for another day. It's all up to you!

Chicken and Stuffing

Prep Time: 10 mins
Cook Time: 25 to 30 mins

2 to 4 Servings

- 1 box (6 ounces) stuffing mix
- 2 cups shredded rotisserie chicken
- 6 ounces frozen peas and carrots
- 1 can (10.5 ounces) cream of chicken (with herbs, if available)
- 5 ounces milk

1 Preheat the oven to 400 degrees.

2 Cook the stuffing according to the package instructions. Set aside.

3 Arrange the chicken in a single layer in the bottom of an 8 × 8-inch baking dish.

4 Pour over the peas and carrots.

5 Mix together the can of cream of chicken soup and milk (fill the empty soup can halfway with milk).

6 Pour the soup mixture over the chicken and vegetables.

7 Spread the stuffing over the top and bake uncovered for 25 to 30 minutes, until golden brown and bubbly.

Cheat Chicken Chili

 Prep Time: 10 mins
Cook Time: 25 mins

 4 Servings

- 1 onion, diced
- 2 tablespoons butter
- 2 cans (4 ounces each) diced green chilies
- 2 cans (15.5 ounces each) white great northern beans, drained
- 1 can (14.5 ounces) sweet corn, drained
- 4 cups chicken stock
- 1 teaspoon ground cumin
- 1 teaspoon garlic powder
- 1 bag (4 ounces) instant mashed potatoes
- 2 cups shredded rotisserie chicken
- Shredded cheddar cheese, cilantro, and diced green onions, for serving

1 In a large saucepan over medium high heat, sauté the onions in the butter until softened.

2 Add the chilies, beans, corn, chicken, stock, cumin, garlic powder, salt, and pepper. Mix well to combine.

3 Once boiling, reduce to a simmer and cook uncovered for about 15 minutes.

4 Stir in the instant potatoes and allow to simmer another 5 minutes.

5 Remove from the heat and let stand to thicken.

6 Serve with cheese, cilantro, onions, and anything else you prefer.

French Onion Chicken Casserole

 Prep Time: 15 mins
Cook Time: 35 mins

 4 to 6 Servings

- 1 cup French onion dip
- ½ cup mayonnaise
- 1 can (10.5 ounces) cream of mushroom soup
- ½ cup cheddar cheese, shredded
- 1 teaspoon garlic powder
- 1 teaspoon onion powder
- Salt and pepper, to taste
- 2 cups shredded rotisserie chicken
- 2 tablespoons butter
- 1 sleeve Ritz crackers, crushed
- 1 cup French fried onions, crushed

1 Preheat the oven 350 degrees.

2 In a large bowl, mix together the French onion dip, mayonnaise, cream of mushroom soup, cheese, garlic powder, onion powder, salt and pepper, and chicken.

3 Bake covered for 20 minutes.

4 Melt the butter and mix together with the crackers and fried onions.

5 Remove the casserole from the oven and add the cracker and onion mixture over the top.

6 Bake uncovered for 15 minutes, until the top is golden brown and casserole is bubbly.

Spinach Alfredo Lasagna Rolls

 Prep Time: 20 mins
Cook Time: 30 mins

 4 to 6 Servings

- 12 lasagna noodles, cooked until al dente, and drained
- 4 ounces cream cheese, softened
- 16 ounces spinach artichoke dip (from the deli section)
- ¼ cup grated Parmesan cheese
- 1 teaspoon red pepper flakes
- 2 cups shredded rotisserie chicken
- 1 jar (22 ounces) alfredo sauce

1 Preheat the oven to 375 degrees.

2 In a bowl, mix together the cream cheese, spinach dip, Parmesan cheese, and red pepper flakes. Once you have this well combined, add the chicken and stir in.

3 Pour about a quarter of the alfredo sauce into the bottom of a 9 × 13-inch baking dish and spread it out.

4 Lay the lasagna noodles flat, and spoon the spinach mixture onto them, spreading it out in an even layer.

5 Roll the noodle up, and lay into the baking dish. This should make about a dozen rolls.

6 Pour the remaining sauce over the top of the rolls. Add a splash of water or milk to the jar, shake and then pour the remainder over. Use a spoon or brush to spread the sauce out.

7 Cover and bake for 30 minutes.

8 Remove from the oven and let stand for about 10 minutes.

Chicken Parmesan Casserole

 Prep Time: 20 mins
Cook Time: 25 to 30 mins

 4 to 6 Servings

- 8 ounces rigatoni pasta, cooked until al dente and drained
- 1 jar (23 ounces) marinara sauce
- 6 ounces shredded mozzarella
- ½ cup grated Parmesan cheese, divided in half
- 2 cups shredded rotisserie chicken
- ½ cup Italian breadcrumbs
- 3 tablespoons butter, melted

1 Preheat the oven to 375 degrees.

2 Mix together the rigatoni, marinara sauce, mozzarella, ¼ cup Parmesan, and chicken.

3 Lightly grease a 9 × 13-inch baking dish with cooking spray and spread the mixture in an even layer.

4 Cover and bake for 15 minutes.

5 Mix together the butter, breadcrumbs, and remaining Parmesan cheese. Spread over the top of the casserole and return to the oven, uncovered, for another 10 to 15 minutes, until golden brown.

Goat Cheese Pesto Pasta

 Prep Time: 5 mins
Cook Time: 20 mins

 4 to 6 Servings

- 8 ounces rigatoni pasta
- ¾ cup heavy cream
- 4 ounces goat cheese, softened
- 3 to 5 ounces basil pesto
- ½ cup sun-dried tomatoes, diced
- ½ cup Kalamata olives, sliced
- Salt and pepper, to taste
- 1 teaspoon red pepper flakes
- 2 cups shredded rotisserie chicken

1 Bring a large pot of water to a boil and cook the rigatoni according to the package directions. Scoop out about a cup of the pasta cooking water, then drain the rigatoni.

2 Return the rigatoni to the pot and stir in the heavy cream and goat cheese until smooth and melted.

3 Add the pesto, tomatoes, olives, salt, pepper, and red pepper. Mix well.

4 Stir in the chicken, and add pasta water, a splash at a time, until you reach the consistency you like. Serve immediately.

Quick Tip: Use any cheese you like! I love goat cheese, so that's what I use. I also love sun-dried tomatoes, so I go a little heavy on those too. Feel free to mix this up and use any ingredients you think would be good.

125

Chicken Pot Pie

 Prep Time: 15 mins
Cook Time: 1 hr

 4 Servings

- 1 can (14.5 ounces) mixed vegetables
- 1 can (10.5 ounces) cream of mushroom soup
- 1 can (10.5 ounces) cream of chicken soup
- Cornstarch slurry (2 tablespoons cornstarch + 2 tablespoons milk)
- ½ teaspoon ground sage
- Salt and pepper, to taste
- 2 cups shredded rotisserie chicken
- 2 refrigerated pie shells
- 1 egg

1 Preheat the oven to 350 degrees. Pull the pie shells out of the fridge and let them sit for about 15 minutes while you get everything ready. This will make them easier to work with.

2 In a large bowl, mix together the cream of mushroom soup, the cream of chicken soup, vegetables, cornstarch slurry, sage, and salt and pepper.

3 Add the chicken and stir to combine.

4 Roll out one of the pie shells and place it into a greased deep pie pan.

5 Add the filling to the pie shell and spread out evenly.

6 Roll out the other pie shell on top, and crimp the edges together with the bottom shell. Trim any excess.

7 Cut a few slits in the top of the pie.

8 In a bowl, scramble the egg with a tiny splash of water. Brush it over the top of the pie shell.

9 Bake for half an hour, then check on the pie. The edges should be starting to brown. Create a pie shield from aluminum foil by folding a square piece in half, then in half again. Cut a circle in the middle and unfold.

10 Cover the edges of the pie with the shield and bake another half hour.

11 Remove from the oven and let stand for about 15 minutes, until the filling has thickened.

Come Fix You a Plate

Here are six of the most popular recipes from my first cookbook, *Come Fix You a Plate*, that was released in April 2023. I never imagined I would sell as many copies as I did, or that I would be here a year later, writing another cookbook. The feedback I received from *Come Fix You a Plate* showed me that there are a lot of people out there just like me, who want to keep our time in the kitchen as easy as possible. I hope you find *Keep It Simple, Y'all* every bit as helpful.

Chicken Cobbler

This was my first viral recipe. I made a couple changes to a similar dish a friend made, and called it chicken cobbler as a joke. The name stuck, and I was even invited to cook it on **Good Morning America!**

 Prep Time: 15 mins
Cook Time: 45 mins

 4 to 6 Servings

- 8 tablespoons (1 stick) butter
- 1 rotisserie chicken, shredded
- 1 bag (12 ounces) frozen vegetables (I use peas and carrots)
- Salt and pepper, to taste
- 2 cups (or one 11.36-ounce box) Red Lobster Cheddar Bay Biscuit Mix
- 2 cups milk
- 2 cups chicken stock
- 1 can (10.5 ounces) cream of chicken soup

1 Place the butter into the middle of a 9 × 13-inch baking dish and place into the oven while it preheats to 350 degrees.

2 Once the butter is melted, remove the pan and add the chicken over the butter in a single layer.

3 Pour the vegetables over the chicken and season to taste with whatever you prefer.

4 Mix together the biscuit mix (including the seasoning packet that comes in the box) and the milk. Pour over the chicken and vegetables. Don't mix it in.

5 In the same bowl you used for the biscuit mix, combine the stock and cream of chicken soup. Pour this over everything in the baking pan. Don't mix it in.

6 Bake uncovered for 45 minutes, then let it stand for 10 to 15 minutes. It will look runny, but will thicken upon standing.

Quick Tip: If you would like to add cheese to the biscuit mixture, go for it! The stock and soup will form a gravy, while the biscuits will separate into little bites of a dumpling consistency. If you'd prefer a more solid crust, reverse the order that you add these to the pan, pouring the biscuit mixture over the top instead.

Chicken and Dumplin's

Before I began teaching myself to cook, this was one of the few dishes I could successfully make. My cousin-in-law suggested using cream of celery soup one day and it was a game changer!

Prep Time: 15 mins
Cook Time: 20 mins

4 to 6 Servings

- 1 box (32 ounces) chicken stock
- 1 can (10.5 ounces) cream of celery soup
- Black pepper, to taste
- 1 can of 8 homestyle biscuits
- 1 rotisserie chicken, shredded

1 Whisk together the chicken stock and cream of celery soup and add to a large pot over medium high heat.

2 While the stock mixture comes to a boil, flour your counter, and roll the biscuits out, one at a time, until thin. Using a knife or pizza cutter, cut them into bite-size squares.

3 By this time the stock should be boiling. Add the biscuits, a handful at a time, and stir in between to coat them fully in the stock.

4 Once they're all in the pot, reduce to a simmer and season however you'd like. I add a generous amount of black pepper to mine.

5 Let the dumplings simmer for 15 to 20 minutes, stirring occasionally.

6 Once they're cooked through, add the shredded chicken and mix together. Let it cook long enough to heat the chicken through.

Cajun't Chicken Pasta

The first time I cooked this on camera, I called it Cajun Chicken Pasta. It went viral, and I was told it wasn't true Cajun cooking, so it has been lovingly referred to as "Cajun't" ever since. I turned the dish into a one-pot meal for this book.

 Prep Time: 15 mins
Cook Time: 40 mins

 2 to 4 Servings

- 4 to 6 slices thick-sliced bacon, diced
- Cajun seasoning of your choice
- 2 to 4 thin sliced chicken breasts
- 1 yellow onion, diced
- Minced garlic, to taste
- A handful of sun-dried tomatoes, chopped
- 2 cups chicken stock
- 1 cup heavy cream
- Black pepper, to taste
- 8 ounces penne pasta (or any short pasta of your choice)
- 4 ounces grated Parmesan cheese

1. Start cooking the bacon in a cold, wide pan over medium high heat. As it heats up, the fat will render out of the bacon. Once it's crispy, remove to a paper towel-lined plate. Leave enough bacon fat to coat the bottom of the pan (a couple tablespoons).

2. While the bacon is cooking, pat the chicken dry and season generously with the Cajun seasoning. Add the chicken to the hot bacon fat and cook for 3 to 5 minutes per side, until cooked through. Remove and set aside.

3. Add the diced onion to the pan and sauté until it begins to soften, about 5 minutes.

4. Add the garlic and sun-dried tomatoes, and cook until fragrant, about a minute.

5. Pour in the stock and cream. Season with black pepper and any other seasonings you prefer.

6. Once the sauce has begun to boil, add the pasta and stir well to coat everything.

7. Reduce the heat to low, and cover. Cook for approximately 12 to 15 minutes, until the pasta is done to your liking.

8. Cut the heat and add the bacon back to the pan along with the Parmesan cheese, stirring well to combine and melt.

9. Slice the chicken breasts on a bias, and serve over the pasta.

Quick Tip: If you'd prefer to dice the chicken into bite-size pieces instead of cooking it whole, just leave it in the pan after browning, and continue on from step 3.

"Really Nice" Salisbury Steak

One evening, when I asked what he wanted for dinner, CJ answered, "I'd love a really nice Salisbury steak." I didn't know exactly what he meant by that, so I threw this together. He loved it, and now this is the dish he requests most often.

Prep Time: 5 mins
Cook Time: 30 mins

4 Servings

- 1 pound lean ground beef
- 1 egg
- 1 tablespoon Worcestershire sauce
- 1 tablespoon mustard (yellow or Dijon)
- 1 packet dry onion soup mix
- ½ cup breadcrumbs
- 2 tablespoons butter
- 2 tablespoons flour
- 2 cups beef stock
- Salt and pepper, to taste

1. In a bowl, combine the beef, egg, Worcestershire sauce, mustard, onion soup mix, and breadcrumbs.
2. Form the mixture into patties. I usually make between 4 and 6 patties.
3. In a wide pan over medium high heat, brown the patties for about 3 minutes on each side. It isn't necessary to cook them all the way through, just long enough to sear and brown the outside.
4. Remove the patties to a plate and set aside. Add the butter to the pan.
5. Once the butter has melted, reduce the heat to low, add the flour, and whisk together. You're making a roux. Continue stirring until the roux darkens to a deep brown color.
6. Add one cup of the stock, whisking vigorously. Once combined and smooth, add the other cup and stir to combine. Season with salt, pepper, and any other seasonings you'd prefer.
7. Once the gravy comes back to a simmer, add the patties, turning them over to make sure they're fully coated. Cover and cook for 10 to 15 minutes, until cooked through.
8. Serve over rice or mashed potatoes and enjoy!

Quick Tip: Use a can of beef consomme and a cup of water in lieu of stock to make the gravy. If you'd like onions or mushrooms in your gravy, add those after you remove the patties from the pan, along with the butter. Sauté until tender, then add the flour and continue following the instructions from that point.

Myrtle's Pasta Bake

I hit the jackpot when it comes to mothers-in-law, and this is the first dish Myrtle cooked for me. My husband comes from a large family, and when someone cooks, they cook enough for everyone. I'm so happy to be a part of it.

Prep Time: 5 mins
Cook Time: 45 mins

4 to 6 Servings

- 1 pound penne pasta
- 1 pound mild Italian sausage links
- 1 can (10.5 ounces) diced tomatoes, drained
- 2 cans (10.5 ounces) cream of mushroom soup
- 8 ounces shredded mozzarella

1   Preheat the oven to 350 degrees.

2   Cook the pasta to al dente, 1 to 2 minutes less than the package instructions. It will finish cooking in the oven.

3   While the pasta is cooking, remove the sausage from the casing, and brown in a pan. While browning, break it into pieces.

4   After the sausage is done, cut off the heat and add the tomatoes and soup. If you'd prefer any additional seasonings, add those now. Stir to combine.

5   Combine the sausage mixture and pasta and mix well.

6   Add half this mixture to a greased 9 × 13-inch baking dish. Sprinkle half the cheese on, then top with the remaining mixture, and finish with the remaining cheese.

7   Bake covered for 25 minutes, and uncovered for an additional 5 to 10 minutes, until the top layer is bubbly.

Quick Tip: If you'd like your pasta to be saucier, add a splash of milk to the mixture. Experiment with it, and after you cook it a time or two, you'll know just how you like it.

CJ's Pork Chops in Onion Gravy

It doesn't matter how many times I cook this dish, it's never quite as good as when CJ does it.

 Prep Time: 5 mins
Cook Time: 90 mins

 4 Servings

- 4 thick-cut boneless pork chops
- Salt and pepper, to taste
- Cajun seasoning of your choice
- Splash of olive oil
- 1 yellow onion, diced
- Minced garlic, to taste (or garlic powder)
- 3 tablespoons butter
- 3 tablespoons flour
- 3 cups chicken stock

1 Season the chops generously with the salt, pepper, and Cajun seasoning.

2 In a wide pan over medium high heat, add just enough oil to coat the bottom of the pan. Sear the chops for 3 to 5 minutes on each side, just long enough to brown them. They don't need to be cooked all the way through. Remove and set aside.

3 Add the butter and onion to the pan, and sauté until the onion begins to soften, about 5 minutes.

4 I added minced garlic as an ingredient here, but we normally just use garlic powder. If you use minced, add it now and cook until fragrant, about a minute.

5 Reduce the heat to low and add the flour to the butter and onions. Stir well and cook until there is no raw flour, a couple of minutes.

6 Add 1 cup of the stock, and once mixed and smooth, add the rest. Stir together.

7 Once the gravy has come back to a simmer, add the chops, turning them over to fully coat them in the gravy.

8 Cook them on a very low simmer for 1 to 1½ hours. They should be fork tender.

Acknowledgments

This book would not exist without my husband, CJ. His love of photography shines in the picture of each dish, and his attention to detail is present on every page. He has patiently accommodated my chaos and lack of schedule throughout this entire process, and I appreciate him more than words can express here. CJ is my rock through this whirlwind that continues to grow; the touchstone that keeps me secure and sane. I love you, babe.

In the fall of 2022, I began posting videos of what I was cooking for dinner online, and found an incredible community that has supported all my endeavors since. I'm no chef, I'm just some guy trying to get food on the table, and you see me for exactly that, and cheer me on endlessly. Together, we've done some pretty cool stuff, like raising money for kids in foster care, buying out wish lists to feed food-insecure children, and supporting small businesses in a big way. I could accomplish none of this without the millions of friends who gather in my kitchen each week. Because of you, this book is possible, and because of you, who knows what the next year holds? Let's go #barefootneighborhood!

Index

B
Beans
    Beef and Rice, 99
    Beef Chili, 49
    Cheat Chicken Chili, 117
    Chicken Tortilla Soup, 39
    Chipotle Lime Chicken Drumsticks, 73
    Italian Chicken with Zesty Veggies, 59
Beef
    and Broccoli, 45
    Chili, 49
    Fajitas, 67
    and Mushroom Risotto, 27
    and Mushroom Stroganoff, 19
    Onion Butter Steak and Potatoes, 101
    "Really Nice" Salisbury Steak, 137
    and Rice, 99
    Smothered Cube Steak and Onions, 35
    Stew, 17
    Taco Taters, 107
Broccoli
    and Beef, 45
    Cheese Orzo, 91
    Kinda Sorta Chicken Alfredo, 89
    Sausage and Gnocchi, 77
    Spicy Peanut Chicken, 79
Brussels sprouts
    Maple Dijon Glazed Chicken, 75
    Parmesan Ranch Pork Chops, 69

C
Carnitas, 41
Carrots
    Beef Stew, 17
    Chicken Stew, 29
    Honey Dijon Drumsticks, 83
Cauliflower
    Honey Dijon Drumsticks, 83
    and Pork Curry, 47
Cheese
    Broccoli Orzo, 91
    Chicken Parmesan Casserole, 123
    Goat, Gnocchi and Meatball Soup, 103
    Goat, Pesto Pasta, 125
    Myrtle's Pasta Bake, 139
    Spinach Alfredo Lasagna Rolls, 121
Chicken
    Alfredo, Kinda Sorta, 89
    BBQ, with Corn on the Cob, 55

Breasts, Cajun Ranch, 81
Cacciatore, 43
Casserole, French Onion, 119
Chili, Cheat, 117
Chorizo Skillet, 87
Cobbler, 131
Coconut Curry, 25
Creamy Mushroom, 13
Drumsticks, Chipotle Lime, 73
and Dumplin's, 133
Goat Cheese Pesto Pasta, 125
Honey Dijon Drumsticks, 83
Honey Garlic, 15
Italian, with Zesty Veggies, 59
Lemon Sun Dried Tomato, 31
Maple Dijon Glazed, 75
Parmesan Casserole, 123
Pasta, Cajun't, 135
Peanut, Spicy, 79
Pita Wraps, 33
Pot Pie, 127
Sausage Pasta, Cajun Ranch, 111
Stew, 29
and Stuffing, 115
Sun-Dried Tomato, 93
Tinga Tacos, 37
Tortilla Soup, 39
Veggie Bake, 61
and Wild Rice, 11
Chili
    Beef, 49
    Cheat Chicken, 117
Corn
    Beef and Rice, 99
    Cajun Ranch Chicken Breasts, 81
    Cheat Chicken Chili, 117
    Chipotle Lime Chicken Drumsticks, 73
    on the Cob, BBQ Chicken with, 55
    Shrimp Boil, 65
Curry
    Coconut, Chicken, 25
    Pork and Cauliflower, 47

E
Eggs
    Breakfast Skillet, 97

F
Fajitas, Beef, 67

G
Gnocchi
    Goat Cheese, and Meatball Soup, 103
    and Sausage, 77

M
Meatball and Goat Cheese Gnocchi Soup, 103
Mushroom(s)
    and Beef Risotto, 27
    and Beef Stroganoff, 19
    Chicken, Creamy, 13
    Chicken Cacciatore, 43
    and Pork Marsala, 23

O
Onion(s)
    and Cube Steak, Smothered, 35
    French, Chicken Casserole, 119
    Gravy, CJ's Pork Chops in, 141

P
Pasta
    Bake, Myrtle's, 139
    Broccoli Cheese Orzo, 91
    Cajun Ranch Chicken Sausage, 111
    Chicken, Cajun't, 135
    Chicken Parmesan Casserole, 123
    Creamy Lemon Shrimp Orzo, 109
    Goat Cheese Pesto, 125
    Italian Sausage Rigatoni, 105
    Kinda Sorta Chicken Alfredo, 89
    Lemon Sun Dried Tomato Chicken, 31
    Spinach Alfredo Lasagna Rolls, 121
    Sun-Dried Tomato Chicken, 93
Peanut Chicken, Spicy, 79
Peppers
    Beef Fajitas, 67
    Chicken Pita Wraps, 33
    Chicken Veggie Bake, 61
    Shrimp and Veggie Stir-Fry, 53
Pineapple
    Coconut Lime Shrimp and Quinoa, 71
    Hawaiian Pork, 21
    and Pork Skewers, 63
Pita Wraps, Chicken, 33

Pork. *See also* Sausage(s)
    Carnitas, 41
    and Cauliflower Curry, 47
    Chops, CJ's, in Onion Gravy, 141
    Chops, Parmesan Ranch, 69
    Hawaiian, 21
    and Mushroom Marsala, 23
    and Pineapple Skewers, 63
    Rice, 95
Potatoes. *See also* Sweet potatoes
    Breakfast Skillet, 97
    Italian Chicken with Zesty Veggies, 59
    Lemon Dijon Salmon and Veggies, 57
    and Onion Butter Steak, 101
    Shrimp Boil, 65
    Taco Taters, 107

Q
Quinoa and Coconut Lime Shrimp, 71

R
Rice
    and Beef, 99
    Beef and Mushroom Risotto, 27
    Chorizo Chicken Skillet, 87
    Pork, 95
    Wild, and Chicken, 11

S
Salmon and Veggies, Lemon Dijon, 57
Sausage(s)
    Breakfast Skillet, 97
    Chicken Pasta, Cajun Ranch, 111
    Chorizo Chicken Skillet, 87
    and Gnocchi, 77
    Italian, Rigatoni, 105
    Myrtle's Pasta Bake, 139
    Shrimp Boil, 65
Shrimp
    Boil, 65
    Orzo, Creamy Lemon, 109
    and Quinoa, Coconut Lime, 71
    and Veggie Stir-Fry, 53
Soups
    Chicken Tortilla, 39
    Goat Cheese Gnocchi and Meatball, 103
Spinach Alfredo Lasagna Rolls, 121
Stews
    Beef, 17
    Chicken, 29
Stuffing, Chicken and, 115
Sweet potatoes
    BBQ Chicken with Corn on the Cob, 55
    Maple Dijon Glazed Chicken, 75

T
Tacos, Chicken Tinga, 37
Tomato(es)
    Chicken Cacciatore, 43
    Sun-Dried, Chicken, 93
    Sun Dried, Lemon Chicken, 31

V
Vegetables. *See also specific vegetables*
    Chicken Cobbler, 131
    Chicken Veggie Bake, 61
    Italian Chicken with Zesty Veggies, 59
    Lemon Dijon Salmon and Veggies, 57
    Shrimp and Veggie Stir-Fry, 53